Book 2

The Book of Expectations

Roscoe Ferris and the Fifth Dimension

Lachlan Cameron

Copyright © 2013 by Lachlan Cameron

All rights reserved. No part of this book may be reproduced in any form or by any means without the prior written permission of the Publisher, excepting brief quotes used in connection with reviews, written specifically for inclusion in a magazine or newspaper.

Contents

Foreword 5

Chapter 1 - Roscoe Ferris 7

Chapter 2 - Welcome to the Fifth 9

Chapter 3 - A New Beginning 17

Chapter 4 - The Return 21

Chapter 5 - Try Again 25

Chapter 6 - Wisdom of the Ages 31

Chapter 7 - Second Chance 35

Postscript   Part 1: Change Your Beliefs 39

Postscript   Part 2: Know that What
                    You Ask For is Already Yours 49

Foreword

Life was not meant to be so hard, and happiness was not meant to be some fleeting sensation. It is time, therefore, that we paid more attention to what we pay attention to.

Nothing is more certain than the knowledge that, as human beings, we can alter our life by altering our attitude; yet for some reason this wisdom lies untouched and unutilized by most in our contemporary society.

We do not attract what we want in life but rather what we are. The task therefore is to change who we are. The problem, of course, is that in order to do this, you have to do the exact opposite to what everyone else is doing. That takes a fair degree of courage.

In the fanciful story of Roscoe that follows, we gain an insight into just how fluid and changing our world could be, and how easy it really is to change our reality if we simply know how.

This book is number two in a series of books that unlock the key to the Hero's journey, the journey that must be undertaken by all great men and women. It touches on one of the seven key steps to transforming what would otherwise be an *ordinary* life into a *remarkable* life. It unlocks one of the keys to being great.

This story is about the power of *Expectation*. It was crafted by Deborah Bremer in the tradition of a fable, and it carries in its light-hearted text great meaning and wisdom. From generation to generation, story-telling has been used as a means to impart wisdom from one generation to the next. This story holds in its narrative powerful and transformative wisdom that we feel compelled to share with the world.

It is possible to be a great person. It is possible to have a great life. It is a choice we encourage you to make, and we invite you to join us on that journey.

Lachlan Cameron

CHAPTER 1

Roscoe Ferris

It was an ordinary Monday morning in late September when Roscoe Ferris turned the corner from the street where he lived in the West Village of New York City and stepped into the fifth dimension.

To say it was a surprise would be inaccurate as well as an understatement.

He stepped from his quite acceptable universe, solid grey concrete sidewalk under his feet, large-sized coffee in his strong pudgy hand, sounds of everyday traffic around him, blue sky above, cool autumn breeze on his face, into a sideways sliding place that was extremely warm, and where he seemed to be slowly rotating in all directions at once.

He was, luckily, a very practical and somewhat small-minded man, and this was a great advantage as he began to flow into the fifth dimension. A more sensitive soul, a person more prone to hysteria, might have literally fallen apart into a million pieces, each piece horrified at the prospect of floating separately through the red sky – or was it the sea, or both? And was that a thousand moons stretching back to eternity? – Poof! The need to comprehend the fifth dimension would overwhelm the newly arrived person, who would then disintegrate. That was common. Roscoe was uncommon in that he held to his plodding beliefs so strongly that it caused him to ignore much about the fifth dimension.

If there was one thing Roscoe believed it was this: there was nothing new under the sun. He often said this. Several people had even given him t-shirts with this slogan on it, because it was so much his known motto. So as he entered a dimension as different from ours as night is from day, he was able to keep his shape, so to speak, because it was what he believed with his whole heart and soul. I am who I am.

The native inhabitants of the fifth dimension were always thrilled to see someone step through the wall and keep his wits about him. It so rarely happened. Usually there was a tear in the wall of being and then a foot appeared, a hand, a face; then all too quickly the person or animal or thought evaporated into nothingness. The inhabitants would notice it and roll their eyes. Roscoe did not disintegrate. Roscoe stood thick and as solid as dull iron.

CHAPTER 2

Welcome to the Fifth

Roscoe Ferris was a welcome addition to the small but happy club of those who survived entrance into the rarified dimension that was known as the "fifth". That name was attributed to Einstein's second mistress. He talked her into many things, and one of them was to plunge her head into the dimension beyond time. She did it, as she was always up for something new, and saw five creatures, each of which was hard to describe when she came back to Einstein's desk. She was in a stunned state and could only whisper, "Five," to Einstein, who took this to mean there was indeed a fifth dimension where multiple realities wove and wafted at will. She actually meant she had seen five creatures, but Einstein, as usual, did not ask her any further questions but went back to his desk and wrote out some new equations. She was mistaken, actually, as there weren't five creatures at all. She had seen five figmented fragments of one creature who was at that moment trying out some new beliefs. Trying, in this dimension, meant for a few moments the "new" idea of oneself would be visible. It helped in the decision-making process to be able to see what one might actually look like or be or feel like if one proceeded with that choice, but we will get to that later. Suffice it to say that Einstein wrote down "fifth dimension," and it stuck.

Roscoe was not imaginative. During his 35 years on earth he had remained primarily static. When he was 22 he had inherited a small studio apartment on Barrow Street from his aunt, and so he moved there from Peoria, Illinois, and found himself a job as a tax examiner for the New York State Government. His life was orderly. He was shy, though not actually reclusive, and he wasn't that smart; but he was very good at looking confident.

The inhabitants of the fifth dimension who were present at his appearing saw a stout younger man, attired in sturdy black shoes, khaki work pants, white shirt and pale green tie with a pattern of leaves on it, wearing a backpack containing his lunch, laptop and vitamins, holding a paper cup full of hot coffee. His hair was cut in a straight line across his forehead so that he looked a little like one of the Beatles from the 1960s.

Roscoe saw a kangaroo with the head of a lion, a beautiful and statuesque woman seated on a throne of ice, and a small otter standing with his hands on his hips, smiling. Roscoe thought to himself, "New York is full of the most interesting people. And animals." He stopped and drank the rest of his coffee. He turned his back because he felt it might be impolite to drink the coffee and not share it with them. He crumpled the cup up and looked for a garbage can. In doing so he was a little disconcerted to see a line of himself in various positions stretching back to the moment when he had stepped into the dimension. Some of the Roscoes were evaporating, some were wandering off, and a couple Roscoes were floating on the ground looking quite happy. As he glanced at this gathering of his selves, he was momentarily flummoxed but then decided it simply didn't exist, and so he turned around and looked out of the corner of his eye at the other three inhabitants.

"And who might you be, stout little man?" the otter said, striding with small but happy steps towards him.

Roscoe looked down and was charmed immediately by the otter's rippling fur and bright smile. Without thinking, and trust me this was the best way to go about an exploration of the *fifth*, he whispered, "Roscoe Ferris." He whispered this very slowly. Roscoe believed that animals had extremely sensitive hearing and were a bit slow on the uptake. This belief took wings, and immediately there was, standing beside the happy otter, another similar otter who was wearing a clumsy hearing aid with a microphone strapped to his chest and a blank look on his face.

"Oh, what a thought," said the happy otter as he looked over the new creation. The new otter quickly froze in one position and then fell backwards and shattered on a pile of white leaves. "Now, let's get on with it. We're so glad to see you! Please come and meet the crew." The otter sauntered over to the gathering of beings who were floating nearby. The kanga-lion and woman were now rotating horizontally just above the otter's head. The otter reached up and pulled them closer. Roscoe stepped back.

"Don't be afraid," shouted the woman as she began to twirl faster on her ice throne.

"Oh, my. Whatever is she doing?" Roscoe whispered to the otter. Once again the dull, hearing-aided otter popped into existence but did not seem capable of speech, so Roscoe turned to the happy otter and said, in a normal voice, "Is she all right?"

The three creatures suddenly shifted and were standing in front of him.

"Oh, he's very adaptable," said the woman. A crown popped onto her head and a staff appeared in her hand. Ah. A sovereign.

"Stout in both tummy and cognitive functions," said the otter.

"He can ignore all non-essential manifestations, and at the same time maintain his shape. Unusual. Reminds me of that two headed snake that appeared sometime late in the last century," the Kanga-lion mused.

"Oh stop. Must you constantly flaunt your length of existence? Does it matter here? Did it matter anywhere?" the Queen snapped.

"It matters to me," Kanga-lion said petulantly.

Roscoe strode up to the throne, as if he were meeting a new client, extended his hand and grasped the Queen's right hand in his. "Hello there. Roscoe. Roscoe Ferris. Very nice to meet you." Her beauty suddenly took hold of him and he blushed deeply as he held her silky hand and gazed into the limitless depths of her eyes. The gaze resulted in his literally falling into her right eye, and it took a moment for him to realize that he'd fallen in and was wafting down into eternity. "Oh dear. This isn't good." He reached for a rope that had suddenly appeared to his left side and was flung with great force out of the eternal downdraft, popped through the Queen's eye socket and fell with very little grace to the forest floor.

"Good Lord," said the Queen, rolling her eyes and blinking quickly to rid herself of the experience. "Please refrain from repeating that unpleasant sensation, my dear. It is discombobulating in the extreme, and I am very much against discombobulation. Also I am against combobulation. I hope that is clear."

Roscoe struggled to a standing position and stood there, somewhat out of breath, looking only at the otter. "So much is not safe," Roscoe observed.

"A truer word was never spoken," said the otter, smiling and nodding his head.

"I must be careful of what I say? And of what I think?" Roscoe asked.

"Of course. Is this any different from your previous existence?" the otter asked.

"My previous existence? You mean where I was the moment before this odd series of events began to unfold?"

"Certainly, Mr. Ferris. Certainly. What world was it? What was its rule of reality?" she asked with warm breath that smelled of peanuts and orange groves.

Roscoe held out his hand and upon it was a tiny diorama of downtown Manhattan, the very street corner where he had last known the world of length, width and depth. Minute taxis careened around the crowded corner, humans jostled, buildings sat firm and sound waves emanated like dust in sunlight. Horns honked, sirens wailed, there was a low murmur of the subway and a host of chattering voices. Roscoe leaned down and blew lightly upon the scene and suddenly it was gone.

"Oh, very elegant. Thank you so much. A visual representation is helpful to one's comprehension as nothing else is. And the sound as well! Delightful!" the otter clapped his paws and hopped up and down a little.

"And you? Have you always been here, little otter?" Roscoe said politely.

The otter produced a small brush and a palette of paint. "Here we go, since you asked so nicely," he said in a tinkling sing-song way. Turning, he began to paint a scene. A small, swift river. High banks. Otters perched. Some jumping in. Fish swimming quickly away. Leaping fish and grasping otters. Sunlight beaming down through massive thick branches. Slowly the vision took form and they were standing together on the grass.

"Oh, isn't that the bee's knees," Roscoe said, sitting down on the bank of the river.

"Go ahead, kick your shoes off," the otter said.

Roscoe carefully removed his black, lace-up, thick-soled shoes and then rolled his black cotton socks down and off. He held them in his lap as he reached down and stuck his toes in the rushing stream.

"You are quite remarkable," said the otter. "I really must say that it has been some time, if time is the word for it, since a creature such as yourself has managed to cross over into our zone and maintained any kind of coherent structure, any kind of consistent belief as it were. Most are gone in a flash; some have time to scream; some manage to keep their heads but their bodies are soon gone, and it is difficult for them to move, so they give up."

"What do you mean, consistent belief?" Roscoe asked, wiggling his toes against the belly of a large silver fish that had come alongside of them.

"Here, in this dimension, this zone, this reality, this concept, this capacity…" The otter took a breath as if to continue in this line of thinking.

"Yes, yes, I understand. Please do go on to the point about belief," Roscoe said firmly.

"Belief. Yes, belief is based upon thought. Not so different from your previous dimensional experience, and yet here it is clearer. The link is immediate. The effect is instant, rapid, snappy, sudden, pretty damn quick, in the twinkling of an eye." He began to speed up, as if to show off his thesaurus-like prowess.

"Yes, yes. I see," Roscoe cut in quickly to stop this flow of patter. "So the belief, what one believes, is what is."

"Was it ever not so?"

"What?"

"Was it ever not so?" the otter said, and looked up with a triumphant smile on his face.

"I suppose it was always so. Here and there. And everywhere," nodded Roscoe. "To believe is to create."

With that, the slippery fish, which had been lying contentedly on Roscoe's cooling toes, leapt out of the water, sprouted wings and was gone in a flash.

"An idea takes flight," Roscoe said ironically.

The otter found this utterly hilarious and began to laugh. His laughter turned into howls and then, as if to put out the fire of humor in his breast, the otter dove into the stream, deep to the river bed, picked up the shining truth that lay there and then wriggled up to the surface of the water and threw it at Roscoe. Roscoe held the truth in his hand for a moment and then, politely, threw it back gently to the otter. They played with the truth for some time, tossing it back and forth, almost losing it but always, at the last moment, grasping at least a bit of its tail. Then the game grew old and they both moved back from the water; Roscoe put his shoes and socks on; the otter shook the water from his fur; and they walked into the forest. A clearing, warmed by several suns (orange, red and yellow), appeared, and Roscoe lay down on the bed for a nap.

As he drifted into peace, the otter leaned down and whispered in his ear, "Here in the fifth, those who flourish have what we call a growth mindset. Nothing is set in stone, darling silly man." A large stone tablet appeared and then turned to gold dust that lightly settled atop Roscoe in the gentlest fashion. "Those with a fixed mindset feel they're stuck with their lot. They cling like babies to a pacifier, hanging on to mediocrity, never moving past low levels of achievement. They do not grow. They freeze in time."

"Oh my. Let's not have that," mumbled Roscoe as he drifted off.

The otter curled up on his feet, and they slept the sleep of contentment.

CHAPTER 3

A New Beginning

It was the Queen, quivering with questions, who woke them. "Here you are! Finally. It took some effort to track you down, I want you to know, some effort." Her powerful voice dripped with exasperation. "I think in fact that I may be sweating."

"That is because," said the otter as he uncurled himself and sat on the side of the bed, "that is because you are not content."

"I certainly am not content and have no intention of being such. However, I know it is your weakness, this contentment, so I searched the world for pockets of untroubled moments, and sure enough, I found the two of you snuggled up in one of the most remote and peaceful locations. Simply asleep under the suns. Doing nothing at all," she bellowed.

"Please stop your bruhahaing," said the otter quietly, "for dear Roscoe is only now stirring from his happy lair."

Indeed, Roscoe was waking. He stretched for a while shaking off the golden dust, groaning happily as one does when one wakes from a very, very nice nap.

"Good heavens to Betsy," snapped the Queen, "whatever do you think you are doing?"

"I believe," Roscoe said, glancing meaningfully at the otter, "I believe I am doing just fine. For what I believe is what is."

"Hmmmph," she said, not convinced. "It seems rather early on for you to be so confident of your ability to maintain a belief, much less manipulate a belief, in this dimension. Perhaps you are simply not very bright."

"This might be true," said Roscoe, "and yet, I wonder if intelligence doesn't lead one to a false sense of confidence? Perhaps belief, the ability to believe firmly, to comprehend the connection between what one believes internally and the external manifestation of it, perhaps belief needs less intelligence and more instinct?"

"I've never heard of anything so idiotic," the Queen said.

"Perhaps I am being unclear," Roscoe said, and he sat thinking for a moment. "When I stepped into this dimension I was momentarily confused, naturally, and my confusion created a multitude of selves, each having a different notion of what was happening. This fragmentation of being is what shatters most who step across. Am I right?"

The Queen reluctantly nodded yes.

"However, oddly, and perhaps this is because my nature has always been rather literal, even to the point of boring and plain, I adapted to this dimension almost instantly. Why is that? I ask myself. Why is that?" Roscoe got up from the bed and spoke to the Roscoe that was coming towards him. "Why is that?"

The second Roscoe began to giggle and quickly melted into a small puddle of glee.

"Well, that wasn't helpful. You see, my dear," Roscoe said, turning to the Queen but being very careful not to fall into her eye, or any other part of her for that matter, "I know that we are what we believe. I know this because I have always believed that there is nothing new under the sun, and so I am solidly content in exactly who I am. As Popeye said, "I yam who I yam.""

"I think therefore I am," piped the otter.

"What I believe is what I become," said Roscoe.

3. A NEW BEGINNING

When Roscoe said this, "What I believe is what I become," a curious and marvelous thing happened. He changed. His physical appearance shifted from the pudgy, sweet, thick-bodied, wide-footed, round-faced Roscoe to a leaner, almost polished, appearance. His hair began to wave and had a new sheen to it. His chest expanded and his waist narrowed. His hips tightened. His feet lengthened and his arch lifted. He raised his left eyebrow and winked at the Queen.

The otter found this bewitching beyond delicious and he literally flipped.

"What I believe is what I become," said Roscoe in a new voice. This voice was not thin but thick, rich, sonorous. His lips softened and reddened. His eyes bore down on the Queen who backed up a step.

"What I believe is what I become" began to have a life of its own, swirling around Roscoe. Sunlight became visible ropes of energy that wove in and out of his limbs, through his shining hair, around his thick, strong neck, down his straight tall back. The sound of oboes and violas, cellos and timpani filled the air. Fireworks exploded overhead. Under their feet, the very ground began to heat and undulate.

"Oh, my," said the Queen as she surrendered to the moment. Her throne appeared and began to crystalize, changing from ice to rock candy as thick, sharp shards of sugar grew, some of them cracking off and crashing on the ground. Clouds of sugar rose from the broken pieces, and slowly the light dimmed, and the throne morphed from an icy brilliance to a warm chocolate.

Roscoe stepped up and sat on a throne of molten chocolate. The smell of melting, rich, sweet chocolate swam out from the chair and filled the air. He lay back and laughed as the throne made room for his body.

The otter, who was watching this with great interest, turned to the audience (that would be us) and said in his most majestic voice, "Change your beliefs. Beliefs drive behavior; behavior drives actions; actions drive results. We see the world as we are, not as it is."

Clearly he was making a point. That point being that in the fifth dimension, and in fact in many dimensions, what we believe is who we are. If we change that belief, then our behavior shifts. When our behavior shifts, different things (actions) take place. Actions lead, inevitably, to results. You no doubt had already surmised that, however, it is my job, humble as it is, to guide you in the paths of knowledge, and therefore... well... enough of that. Let us return to Roscoe and see what happened next.

CHAPTER 4

The Return

From the melting, creamy chocolate throne, the firm and increasingly handsome Roscoe rose and strode forward. Little strands of chocolate flowed behind him like a cape. With confidence he ran towards the stream, which now had grown into a great, whirling dark river, and dove in head first. The stream carried him swiftly away, and soon he was cresting a high waterfall that plunged a thousand feet into the wet, hot jungle. Deciding not to take the fall, he flew, on the wings of a friendly dove, out across the vast tangled jungle, out across the empty lands of grey sand and yellow boulders, out across the fields of wheat waving in the summer sun, out across the blue sea teaming with schools of tangerine fish, out across the surface of a massive dirty white glacier, and up to the highest peak in the fifth dimension, carved by time into the head of a peacock. There he perched, left by the dove, holding onto the fragile sculpture for dear life.

It was at this moment that someone – perhaps a writer with too large an imagination, perhaps a passing mother who saw him struggling to hold on, perhaps a little boy who thought he was an action figure; we aren't sure – but at that moment, someone reached a hand through from the corner of Barrow Street and Hudson Avenue in the West Village of Manhattan and jerked Roscoe back into the blaring, comfortable, busy world from which he had so recently fallen.

Roscoe Ferris stood still and thought for a moment.

"What do I believe?" he said to himself. Then he made a decision that he would believe that *all things were possible*. With that he stepped forward, a taller, happier Roscoe, walking swiftly, smiling broadly, thinking grand thoughts and clutching a paper cup full to the brim of hot chocolate.

BECOME.
Become today what it is you desire.

Roscoe stepped cheerfully through the morning crowds, rubbing elbows with very elbowy people. Jostled here and there, he held his coffee cup over his head in order to retain all the lovely hot bean-drenched water. This was not effective, however, and so he arrived at the office with a spray of brown liquid across his white shirt, and a brown riverlet ran down the center of his pale green tie.

"Yes... well now... good morning," Roscoe said to the receptionist.

She glanced up and gave him an up-and-down glance in the way women do with men of whom they are unsure.

"Spilled a little coffee, not a problem, not a problem!" he blurted out. She looked down at her smart phone, hoping for a text. He stood there for a minute, watching the morning light lying on her hair. Lush, dark, dirty-blond hair, falling in waves over her shoulders and half-way down her back. By the flat black phone sat a warm almond croissant. He took a deep whiff and his eyes watered ever so slightly because of his undying, unknown, unexpressed love for her. She ate an almond croissant, warm, covered with powered sugar, every morning. The smell had become her presence. When she went on vacation, he would buy a similar croissant and put it in his desk drawer and throughout the day, when no one was near, he would open the drawer, lean his head down and breathe in the aroma of almond groves, fields of butter, a seashore of white sugar, and so on. Today she was here, in all her shining glory, and he almost reached out and took her large hand in his. But no. No. He knew, and had always known, that it was not to be. That it would never be.

He whispered these words to himself, "Never be," over and over as he walked down the long, bare-walled hallway and into his real life. The moment he sat in his desk, he forgot about her. This happened every day. Every day for the last six years. Bliss. Despair. Forget about it. As he settled into the outline of his own body, which had been pressed into his office chair hour after hour after hour after hour, he took a breath and got on with it.

Almost. There was a moment, brief but vivid, when he felt a part of himself peel off, in a fifth-dimension kind of way, and run back down the hall towards her. Before that part reached her, however, it tripped and smashed into a billion pieces right there on the carpet and sank into the floor like ground-in dirt. A voice whispered in his mind, majestic and hopeful, "Change your beliefs!"

"Oh dear," he said as he held his breath for a moment, remembering the experience of the past however long it was since he had fallen into the fifth dimension and then returned. "Oh dear."

She was dear. She was his dear one. She had a rather large nose and large hands, and her eyes were far apart. He liked her sizes. "Now, now. What belief is there to change? That she would love me?" Roscoe shook his head. "No. I can change some beliefs. For instance, I will change the side of my desk where the phone has always sat." This he did. He was surprised to see the shiny surface where the phone had been sitting for the last decade. The rest of the desk was dull. He knew that in order to be successful in going forward, he needed to do the exact opposite of his past frozen and mediocre instinct.

"That is enough to start with. It's quite different," he said, picking the phone up awkwardly with his left hand. "I'll have enough to grapple with. This is a change that will take some getting used to."

CHAPTER 5

Try Again

At that moment, in the fifth dimension, the Queen, the otter and the Kanga-lion were leaning up against the wall that thinly divided their worlds, ears pressed to the border of realities, and they let out a collective "Augh!" The Queen, in fact, was so disgusted with Roscoe's return to small-minded struggle that she reached through the dimension and was about to smack Roscoe on the head when the otter poked her under the arm and told her to mind her own business. With a shriek, she pulled her arm back in, only to find it had turned into a fax machine.

Trying a second time, she managed to grab Roscoe by the left ear and hauled his head into the fifth dimension. There he was, leaning forward with no head visible. Sadly, no one walked by to see this curiosity. On the other side, the Queen was nose-to-nose with Roscoe.

"Look here, you silly little man!" she began. "Must we make everything so clear to you?"

"Well, yes, that would be helpful," Roscoe said.

"Oh," the Queen answered. "Well, why not? Listen, what you do not understand is this – you will get what you are. Do you understand that?"

Roscoe said, "No."

"What you seek," she said loudly, "is already yours."

"Oh, I can't imagine that!" Roscoe answered.

"Exactly! You're vibrating on a frequency of inadequacy and doubt. If you could manage to have the slightest grain of faith, be it only a fleck or speck, you would find that what you want, what you believe and have faith in, can be yours."

"Subconscious," the otter chanted, "sub-sub-sub-sub-conscious."

"Be quiet," the Queen ordered, but the otter continued chanting and doing one-armed push-ups. "Have faith. See it in your mind. Imagine it in your hands. Know that it is there and that it is yours."

The otter stopped chanting and said to her, "Good Lord, that's quite smart of you. Very articulately expressed. I can't imagine he will comprehend it, but it was worth a try, I suppose."

"Your Blueprint is all wrong," continued the Queen.

"My what?" asked Roscoe, now a little confused.

"You and all your pudgy pale kind have a blueprint embedded in your subconscious mind. It's been there since you were a child and it's what makes you all so dull. It will continue to determine your destiny for the remainder of your life unless you intervene. You will never grow beyond the confines of the blueprint you have subconsciously set for yourself. Like the thermostat on a heater, once you reach your set point, you will shut off. You simply need to turn up the thermostat, my dumpy dear."

The Queen and her court looked at Roscoe for quite a while. There was, as they say, a deep silence. And then there was an uncomfortable silence. Finally the Queen took her large brass scepter and pushed Roscoe's head back into his normal world. Roscoe ran his hands over his head and then went back to doing practically nothing.

"That was effective," the otter said. Kanga-lion giggled.

The Queen snapped her fingers, and a small creature appeared – an unusual little man of unexpected appearance, wielding a

5. TRY AGAIN

bow and arrow. Smiling widely, she leaned down and whispered into the little thing's ear.

"Shoot him?" the thing said.

"In the heart!!!!" the Queen shrieked.

Otter and Kanga-lion allowed their eyes to pop briefly out of their heads.

"Oh, stop that, I've done it a thousand times, well, maybe four or five times. I don't remember. Colonel Sanders, Warren Buffet, Walt Disney, blustery Henry Ford – all limpid, odd failures until I taught them. And let's not forget William James and all we taught him. How wise he appeared to the dim-witted lot they are when he pronounced, 'The greatest discovery of my generation is that a human being can alter his life by altering his beliefs.' Well, who do you think taught him that? Besides, look at some of the ones we decided not to help and what they ended up believing!"

Clouds flew by with the following quotations imprinted upon them in azure stones.

"Flight by machines heavier than air is unpractical, if not utterly impossible."

Simon Newcomb – Astronomer – 1902

"Sensible and responsible women do not want to vote."

Grover Cleveland – 1905

"Who the hell wants to hear actors talk?"

Harry Warner – Warner Brothers – 1927

> *"I think there is a world market for about five computers."*
>
> Thomas J. Watson - Chairman of IBM - 1943

> *"There is no reason for an individual to have a computer in their home."*
>
> Ken Olsen - President Digital Equipment - 1977

"Oh, my, nicely done," said the otter, rolling his eyes from one side of his face to the other. He turned and whispered loudly to Kanga-Lion, "She really is so obvious sometimes. Why must she go on about how how how how how how?"

"I'm on a mission! It must be done!" The Queen howled and stomped her foot, causing several earthquakes in lower Tasmania.

With a nod of her head the Queen propelled the little man and his bow and arrow out of the fifth dimension and into the world of Roscoe Ferris.

Roscoe was in one piece, at his desk, pondering, when suddenly a burst of wind and rain blasted like gravel on glass, causing Roscoe to leap up from his usual position and peer out into what had been a plain-weather day. He stood looking out the window when suddenly, nose to nose, he found himself peering into the tiny eyes of a tiny man. Just as Roscoe was beginning to form a coherent thought about who this creature might be, the tiny hands of the tiny man pulled out a... yes .... a tiny arrow and shot it right through the glass. Shattering the glass and piercing the white shirt and thick pale skin, between two thick ribs and into the heart of Roscoe Ferris flew the arrow. And there it stuck.

5. TRY AGAIN

Well, Christopher Columbus in a pink bunny outfit. This was the second surprise of the day, if you don't count changing the phone from side to side, and one really can't count that. In through the heart the arrow flew, and Roscoe, with a gurgling gasp, fell through the now shattered window.

The Queen let out a great cheer from her throne in the fifth dimension and then said, "That'll get him going in the right direction! Nothing like a little challenge."

The otter rolled his eyes and said under his breath, "If he lives..."

Naturally, the Queen did not let him die but jerked him, with great skill, back into the fifth dimension and directly over a pond of dark, swampy water.

When Roscoe entered the pond, his first thought was, "Warm water," and his second thought was, "I think I will close my eyes because I'd rather not see what happens next." So with his eyes closed, he began to tumble in slow, watery motion down and around. He felt something fluffy, like seaweed, brushing by his skin, and then small, soft, claw-like things started grabbing him ever so lightly and pushing him this way and that way. There was a sudden sound of, he wasn't sure what as he had not heard it before, perhaps bells under water?

Slowly he sank to what felt like the bottom. The bells continued along with the furry wet things, and the little claws kneaded his body like a kitten trying to extract milk from its mommy. He opened his eyes. Everything was dark. He had no need to breathe and assumed, in his Roscoe kind of way, that he was now dead and therefore not in need of oxygen. He lay there for a while and then felt himself lifted up by the little claws and, with a great rush of power, he was thrust forward and right out of the pond, although it was the bottom of the pond, and into a layer of time and space that lay directly under his world. It was dark and cool, but light streamed through at various places and showed a vast landscape, unpeopled.

The claws were small hands, the bells burst into laughter, and he was holding onto great wings, great flapping wings. He was being held and flown by a flock of angels, a great mass of joy and happiness winging its way collectively and individually through time and space.

Those watching from the fifth dimension viewing platform let out a collective gasp. *"Oh my, gigantic angels!"* or *"Who ever talked them into it?"* or *"I thought they were above such things."* The gathered group looked over at the Queen.

The Queen furrowed her brow and declared, "They owed me one!"

The small crowd looked at her with disbelief and then began to mutter quietly things like, *"I seriously doubt that,"* and, *"More likely they were passing by and had nothing better to do,"* and, *"Such delusions of grandeur she has; it becomes worse every century."*

Roscoe wiggled in their grasp as he looked at them. They had faces of every color and shape. There was one made of chalk, one of black marble, one of clear honey, one that looked like an oatmeal cookie, one that was pale and had a rather large nose. He looked at that one for a long time. The large nose one. (Yes, it has an obvious connection to the receptionist, but that is what happened in the story, and we can't control the twists and turns of such things.)

They were, of course, *Principalities*, a type of angel that, well, it is complicated to explain. Suffice it to say they were angels of a very high and mighty order and they were merely carrying out the orders of a certain *Dominion* that had taken a liking to the ways of men. As was their habit, they thought it was a great happy lark, and flapped cheerfully across a dark underground mountain range.

CHAPTER 6

Wisdom of the Ages

As he was flying forward at a great speed, Roscoe glanced down and saw the arrow sticking out of his coffee-stained white shirt. A trickle of blood ran down his shirt pocket. He felt no pain, however, and then remembered that he was most likely dead. This was an oddly relaxing thought until he caught sight of the big-nosed angel, and his eyes filled with tears. There would be no love now. Just as he had always believed. Normally this would have comforted him, as he preferred things to stay the same, and yet in this moment, he did not feel comfort or peace. In this moment he suddenly knew the part of him that wanted to run back down the long bleak hall and stand at her desk and tell her a joke and see her laugh. He wanted to bring her half-decaf/half-regular coffee with sugar and then sit in the chair by the desk and listen to her tell him about something funny that had happened on the subway that very morning. Then they would pause and look out the window and feel that lightness of spirit that comes when love is given away and enjoyed. And part of him wanted to do so much more than sit at that desk not thinking. He wanted to create, inspire and build tall buildings. Despair overtook him as he glanced over his shoulder at the life he had wasted.

The pack of Principalities were slowly moving down and drifting in a great fluffy, happy, giggly mass onto a tree. They perched, yes, like a flock of blackbirds, but they were multicolored: some were beyond color and some were the opposite of color, which is hard to explain but it does exist. Not to get side-tracked, they perched, and he with them.

Roscoe was crumpled in the lap of one of them. Crumpled sideways, sticking up at an odd angle because of the arrow in his chest that protruded about two inches out of his back and two inches out of his front. The Principality leaned down and pulled the arrow out, and then blew on poor Roscoe, who was about to scream bloody murder. She or he or whatever, let's say IT, IT blew warm, bubbly air onto him, and suddenly everything was all right. Even the coffee stain went away. His psoriasis vanished. The gaping hole in his chest was no longer an issue.

IT looked down at him with a large grin. IT did not have teeth, but when IT grinned, little upside-down umbrellas opened in its mouth, and it was really quite a pleasant sight.

One by one the huge angels leaned down and whispered in his ear. This is a rough translation of what they said:

There is always hope. Desire to do and be more. Become that desire. Believe it. Then start to work for it. Risk and Act and Risk and Act. There is always hope. Also, eat an apple a day.

Roscoe listened intently and the words became divinely engraved upon the tablet of his brain. "Thank you," he said.

The Principality looked very surprised, shrieked and threw him out of IT's lap. IT flew away exclaiming, "Lo, The Creature Speaketh!"

Evidently, the angels weren't often around polite people who expressed their thanks properly. It was a shock, a happy one of course, as all things were for the angels.

He fell down through the tree, his downward spiral slowed by the hands and wings and well-meaning warm breathing of the angels. Down he fell and then ever so gently, ever so quietly, he landed in a small mud puddle.

There he sat, in the realm of glory, once again stained.

He barely noticed. He did not notice at all, in fact. What he was thinking in this moment was, "There is always hope – I surprised an angel."

That thought, that rare and blessed thought grew quickly, like bamboo in a sped-up film showing how quickly bamboo grows; the thought grew into an epiphany.

The epiphany was, "If there is always hope, then I can do almost anything. Almost anything in the world. I am capable. I am capable of becoming whatever I want. Whatever I desire. I, Roscoe Ferris," and with this he stood up in the middle of the small mud puddle, "do say in this moment that I am capable of becoming whatever I desire to become."

The remaining perched Principalities look down at him with beaming eyes. There was a blast, like from trumpets or like the wheels of cars screeching around the sharp bend in the racetrack, and Roscoe watched as the entire choir of Principalities jumped out of the tree and took to the air. They flew in a weaving way, like a dance but not quite planned, in and out of each other's space, some flying backwards, some upside down and the rest just regularly flapping forward. He was left alone. Under the great tree and warm sun.

He was hungry.

CHAPTER 7

Second Chance

He started to walk, to walk down a path, and as his belief took hold, his belief that what he longed for and needed and wanted was already his, the path morphed into a hallway, actually, a long hallway, and at the end was a desk. And at the desk was a dirty blonde. Was it all so predictable? Only if you started the story with hope. (And that right there is a good lesson. Start with hope and maybe you won't be surprised. You'll just go from delight to delight.)

And in front of the dirty blonde with the big nose were two warm almond croissants.

She looked up.

"Hi," Roscoe said, his eyes filling with tears.

"Are you all right?" she said, her brow suddenly furrowed, leaning forward almost standing to see if he was hurt.

He considered saying, "Yes, considering I was just shot through the chest with an arrow, drowned in a pond, dragged underground by a great herd of angels, flown at great speed to a tree where one of them freaked out and threw me into the air, and then I landed in a mud puddle."

But he did not say this. What he said, in that glorious moment, was the thing that he had desired to say for the last six years, and that was, "I'm all right now. Now that I am here. Now that I am here," (long pause) "with you."

The Queen watched all this as she was eating pineapple pizza and she let out a burp and then said, "I am effectiveness incarnate.

We do not get what we want, we get what we are. I taught another dull, silly little human how to change what he is and therefore change what he gets. Now, let us move on to more interesting things." With that, she shot directly up into the sky, as if she had been sitting in an ejector seat. Pop. The rest of her court began to pop up with her, and they receded far into the night sky. On to other adventures.

Roscoe Ferris leaned forward and looked at what was already his. The desire to love was now manifest in his reality. He was what he desired. He was a man who could change and love and thrive and seize the day.

The Queen couldn't resist and popped her head back one last time. In all honesty, she had not enjoyed herself this much in quite some time. She had taken something of a liking to this tubby little man, although she would never admit it to any creature real or imagined.

"Don't forget the agenda," she said to her new protégé.

"What's the agenda?" Roscoe asked.

The Queen tore her head back and looked the otter squarely in the eyes with a glare of such wrath the poor little otter staggered backwards and fell over his own flippers.

"Well," the otter stammered, "he wasn't here all that long. We didn't have time for everything."

"The agenda, my dear," she continued, placing her head back into Roscoe's world, "and I shall only say it once more, is simple, even for you."

The otter groaned loudly and mouthed to Kanga-Lion, "Seriously, she is the most obvious of the obvious. Let the poor man learn it for himself... but no... she must have her lecture."

The Queen stood at a large, wooden lectern, wearing a black academic robe. Using a power point presentation, she taught the following agenda to dear Roscoe, and through him to the world in general.

Love and be loved.
Make your work a gift to the world.
Maintain a healthy Mind, Body and Soul.
Be financially free.

"You may have mastered love, but it's time you turned your attention to the other three. After all, you could lose a pound or two."

The scene began to fade and Roscoe was there, frozen over the croissant, his fingers lightly touching the receptionist's.

"And what was that?" she asked in a small but panicked voice.

"Oh, the Queen?"

"Is it, was it, a Queen?" She looked up at him with such need that he took her hand and gently held it.

"Yes. I will tell you all about it."

"Don't you want the croissant?"

"Not just now. There is too much to do. We will discuss it over dinner. I must go now and find a better job, do some exercise and get going with my rare and wonderful life. I'll pick you up after work and we will ... we will begin."

"Oh, that'll be nice," she said, looking up at a stronger, happier, man whom she had always believed would show up some day. And here he was.

There is always hope once *expectation* takes hold and follows desire.

THE END.

Postscript

Part 1: Change Your Beliefs

The fanciful story of Roscoe and the Fifth Dimension is a humorous way of approaching the revelation that we can actually change our beliefs, and as a consequence – our world will change. Roscoe enters a world where indeed the very act of thinking produces instant results. Our world is not as fluid or ridiculous, and yet it is clear in our own world of more solid objects that what we think, and what our attitude is, ultimately becomes reality.

The idea that we can alter our lives by altering our attitude is such an empowering concept. *We*, not others, not circumstance and not external influences, can alter our own life. This is what Roscoe ultimately learns through his falling into a world where reality changes in the blink of an eye.

A human being can alter his life by altering his attitudes.

As children we are born with what you might call a "success" mindset. It's what induces us to walk and talk despite the enormous effort, setbacks and difficulty involved. Nonetheless, for most of us, this "success" mindset is lost at some point in the process of growing up. Roscoe is a prime example of this. He has settled for less than he wants or dreams of.

> *Successful people believe
> nothing is set in stone.
> Who they are and where they are in life
> can always be changed
> with dedication and effort.*

The good news is that the "success" mindset of which we speak is little more than a set of attitudes and knowledge that anyone can adopt and acquire. Anyone, that is, who makes a commitment to do so. Most people do not, of course, which is why it is not all that difficult in life to separate yourself from the herd and achieve the life that 99% of the population would like but do not achieve.

Most of us are simply the product of our environment. We learn our beliefs from others – parents, friends – and adopt them in our own life. The problem, of course, is that we have a 99% chance of getting it wrong. To be successful we need to understand what successful people do and how they do it, and then we need to copy them.

> *In order to be successful you have to do the exact
> opposite of what most other people are doing.*

The biggest hurdle that stands between most people and the achievement of significant sustainable health, wealth and happiness is their set-in-stone way of thinking or their beliefs. Beliefs lead to feelings, feelings lead to actions, and actions lead to results.

You need to change the way you think. Frankly, this is less difficult or taxing than you might think. It does require you to adopt a new way of seeing things, a new set of beliefs and a new understanding of what you perceive to be reality. For most people, this is a challenge, and as a consequence, they remain stuck in mediocrity. For those willing to make the change, a new world awaits and their efforts will be richly rewarded. Like Roscoe, you might shed the skin of a mediocre life and reach out to what you really want.

By influencing our actions, beliefs ultimately determine our success and prosperity. For the great majority of the population – that is, the 95% who are not wealthy or the 99% who are not Healthy, Wealthy and Happy – their beliefs generate self-defeating or self-limiting thoughts and habits that continually inhibit the transformation process.

A number of influences shape our beliefs – what we hear, what we see and what we experience. The truth is, we actually see the world as *we* are, not as *it* is. Roscoe saw himself as a small-minded man, and so that is what he became. When he began to expand his idea of himself, so his life expanded. When he changed, the world changed.

> We see the world as we are,
> not as it is.

Your old ways of thinking and acting have brought you to where you are right now in life. Most people do not reach their full potential; most people are not successful. The wealth, success or happiness you have, or do not have, is a direct result of the actions you have taken and the beliefs you hold. A lack of money, or health or happiness is merely a symptom of what is going on underneath.

Each of us each of us already has a personal money and success blueprint embedded in our subconscious mind. In many cases, it has been there since the age of seven or eight. As ridiculous as it sounds, it is this blueprint, more than anything and everything else combined, that will determine your financial destiny.

> Each of us each of us already has a personal money and success blueprint embedded in our subconscious mind. It is this blueprint, more than everything else combined, that will determine our financial destiny and success.

What makes this particular area of personal transformation more complicated than most is the fact that so many of our beliefs are in fact subconscious and therefore often not always apparent.

> When the subconscious mind must choose between deeply rooted emotions and logic, emotions will almost always win.

This blueprint and your beliefs around money and success are first formed when you are a child. They continue to determine your destiny unless you intentionally intervene and revise these beliefs.

So how do we change? The first step is AWARENESS – you must first identify current beliefs before you can begin to change. The next step is UNDERSTANDING – by understanding why you held such beliefs, you can begin the process of acceptance and disassociation. The next step is DISASSOCIATION – this is where you recognise the harm this belief is causing you, the need to change and the ease with which you can change, given that it was not really your belief in the first place but rather something you inherited from another. Finally there is ADOPTION – this is where you adopt a new and significantly more useful belief to replace the old.

Keep in mind that this need not be a drawn-out procedure. Change can be an extremely quick process if the new paradigm strikes an intuitive chord. You are capable of moving through Awareness, Understanding, Disassociation and Adoption in an instant when presented with something that resonates.

The idea that you can instantly change your beliefs without struggle or hardship is a powerful thought indeed and it strikes at the core of what makes the human race so special. We may perceive our world and our selves to be firm and unchanging, and yet we are more like Roscoe's fifth dimension than we might think.

We are not merely instinctive creatures. While our upbringing and past experiences may influence our beliefs, they do not determine them. We have a discerning mind and can therefore use free will to choose our thoughts and not be purely instinctive.

> *You can change your belief through a process of Awareness, Understanding, Disassociation and Adoption. Furthermore the process of change can be instant. While our upbringing and past experiences may influence our beliefs, they do not determine them.*

For most of us, it is time we began to express this unique human endowment and change some of the most common limiting factors we face in the attainment of significant and sustainable wealth.

The following is a summary of the key beliefs that either keep us poor (THE POOR) or take us on the first step towards becoming rich (SUCCESS).

SUCCESS	THE POOR
Abundance. There is plenty for everyone. Those who are successful believe there is plenty for everyone. Trillions of dollars circulate the world each day. You just need to stick your hand out to catch your piece of it.	**Lack.** Money doesn't grow on trees. The Poor believe there is a scarce quantity of resources to go around. One person's gain is another person's loss.
There is no need to work hard forever. Those who are successful value time, not money, so they constantly look for ways to work smarter not harder. Those who are successful realise that becoming rich and happy requires no more effort than being poor. They only need to work hard until their money works harder.	**Need to work hard.** The Poor believe you must work hard to get on in life. Therefore they trade their time for money. The Poor believe becoming rich requires a great deal of effort, and they are not willing to make that commitment.
You deserve to be rich and happy. Those who are successful believe that desire is good and they deserve the best life can offer. It is natural and a healthy aspect of human nature to desire more. Money will help provide a richer, fuller life.	**Money doesn't make you happy.** The Poor believe it is wrong to want more. We should be happy with what we have. They feel they do not deserve to be wealthy and happy when there is so much misery and unhappiness in the world.
You have only one life. Those who are successful do not separate their work life and home life – it is one life. They seek to achieve a good balance on average, not on a daily basis.	**You need to juggle work and home life.** The Poor only work Monday to Friday 9am to 5pm. They only allocate time to their home life outside of these hours.

SUCCESS	THE POOR
You are in control. Those who are successful believe they are the architects of their lives. They are in control. The life they achieve will be a direct result of their actions and beliefs.	**Circumstance determines your life.** The Poor believe they are pawns in the great game of life; they believe they have limited control over what happens to them.
Admire the success of others. Those who are successful admire other rich and happy people. Their success only confirms that they too can achieve their goals.	**Resent the success of others.** The Poor are suspicious of rich and successful people, and dubious regarding how it is they have achieved such success.
You will not be held back by lack of talent. Those who are successful know that becoming rich and happy requires no great talent. It is not complex, and anyone with a normal level of intelligence can achieve health, wealth & happiness.	**Lack of talent.** The Poor believe they do not have the talent necessary to be rich.
Do not rely on savings alone. Those who are successful know that while saving is important, becoming Rich is more about investing.	**Focus on saving.** The Poor focus on saving. They never overcoming their fear of investing and never develop the necessary skills.
You are not limited by your profession or business. Those who are successful understand that becoming rich and happy does not require them to engage in a particular profession or business. There are many avenues open to them.	**Believe they are in the wrong profession or business.** The Poor believe the reason they are not rich is that they are in the wrong profession or business.

SUCCESS	THE POOR
You will not be held back by your lack of capital. Those who are successful understand that becoming rich does not require Capital as a starting point.	**Allow the lack of capital to hold them back.** The Poor blame a lack of capital or the fact that they are currently poor for their inability to ever become rich.
Wealth is not just for the wealthy. Those who are successful know that the wealth creation process is a process and does not favour one person or one class over another.	**The Poor can never be Rich.** The Poor believe the wealth creation process favours the wealthy over the working class.
Success is an exact science. Those who are successful understand that the process of becoming rich and happy is an exact science that, if followed, makes failure impossible.	**Those who are successful are lucky.** The Poor believe those who are successful are lucky. They do not accept that the process of becoming rich is an exact science that, if followed, makes failure impossible.
Becoming successful need not take a long time. Those who are successful understand that the process can be rapid if you identify a need and can help others achieve their goals.	**Wealth creation takes more time than I have available.** The Poor believe that the wealth creation process takes more time than they have available.
Those who are successful play to win. Those who are successful focus on what they want. They commit themselves to an outcome, and failure is not an option.	**The Poor play not to lose.** While the Poor would like to be rich, they feel that it is more important not to be poor. As a consequence, they avoid risk and seek certainty.
Success is made mentally before it appears physically. Those who are successful know that "You'll see it when you believe it."	**I'll believe it when I see it.** The Poor will not believe it until they see it, and as a consequence, they will never see it.

SUCCESS	THE POOR
The world is already perfect. Those who are successful accept that the world is already perfect. That good and bad will always exist, just as night and day are the opposite sides of the same coin. They do not attempt to change the world, just themselves.	**The world is a terrible place.** The Poor focus on what's wrong with the world. They spend time and energy trying to change things that are already as they should be and will always be.
Competition is bad. Those who are successful avoid competition. They always look for a way they can be different, to provide a different product or service, to satisfy an unsatisfied want or need.	**Competition is good.** The Poor believe that it is okay to compete. They work in businesses or start companies that compete with others.
Love the plateau. Those who are successful recognise that life is not a series of endless climaxes in short successive progression. They recognise that success comes with patient, long-term effort and the creation of value in return.	**Hate the plateau.** The poor believe life should consist of one climax after another, and that these new heights can somehow be reached without extensive instruction and discipline.
The world is impermanent. The successful no longer cling to the idea of permanence in a world that is inherently impermanent. Change is constant. You need to learn to go with the flow of change rather than try to stop change from occurring.	**See the world as stable and permanent.** Those who are unsuccessful try to slow change and maintain the status quo. They see the forms and phenomena of the world to be real and permanent.

SUCCESS	THE POOR
I am limitless. The successful identify with their true being. They recognise that they are connected to all that exists; they have no limitations; they have infinite creativity; they are fearless and willing to step into the unknown trusting that their intention can become reality.	**I am a physical being.** The unsuccessful crave approval and fear disapproval because it diminishes their self-image. They identify with objects outside themselves. They need outside validation in order to belong and have worth. They feel limited and bound; without power and control over others, they feel helpless and exposed. They prefer routine and habit over creativity. They find security in making today the same as the day before. They fear the unknown more than anything else because they see the unknown as a place of darkness and emptiness. They struggle to acquire what they want and assume that without struggle, their needs would never be fulfilled. This reflects a deep sense of inner lack.

Postscript

Part 2: Know that What You Ask For is Already Yours

Those who are truly successful know that what they ask for is already theirs. They don't believe, they don't hope, they don't pray, they know! Not at some point in the future, not soon, but now, it is already theirs! Sure, maybe not physically, but that's just detail.

When you place a clear and concise request via your commitment to a desire, your desire has already been delivered in the non-physical world; it now simply needs to come about in the physical world. What you seek is already here; it has just not arrived in a physical sense.

All creations are created twice, first in your mind and then – and only then – in the physical form. This is a natural law, and just like gravity, it works every time. All creations start as an idea. For this idea to become a reality, the creation must be developed in one's mind to a point where you can touch, smell and feel this object even if at this point it is only imagined. Behind your purpose must be an invincible and unwavering faith that the thing is already yours, that it is "at hand". The fact that you are yet to take possession of it is mere detail – splitting hairs, unnecessary scepticism.

> Behind your commitment to achieve Wealth,
> Health and Happiness
> must be an invincible and unwavering FAITH
> that what you desire
> is already yours – that it is "at hand" and you
> have only to take possession of it.

We need to articulate our creation clearly, to the point where it becomes a reality. We need to imagine how it looks and feels. We need to imagine ourselves interacting with this object or lifestyle. We need be grateful for the joy and benefits it brings, even if it is yet to become a physical reality.

In the mental or non-physical realm, you must enter at once into full enjoyment of the things you want. See the things you want as if they were actually around you all the time; see yourself as owning and using them. Make use of them in imagination just as you will use them when they are your tangible possessions. Dwell upon your mental picture until it is clear and distinct, and then take the Mental Attitude of Ownership towards everything in that picture. Take possession of it, in mind, in the full faith that it is actually yours. Hold to this mental ownership; do not waver for an instant in the faith that it is real.

Live in your new life, mentally, until it takes form around you physically. Enter at once into full enjoyment of the things in this new life, see yourself as owning and using them. Make use of them in imagination just as you will use them when they are your tangible possessions. Dwell upon your mental picture until it is clear and distinct, and then take the Mental Attitude of Ownership towards everything in that picture. Take possession of it, in mind, in the full faith that it is actually yours. Hold to this mental ownership; do not waver for an instant in the faith that it is real.

Your mind must be dominated by positive emotions – refuse to think about negative things. Negative thoughts may float through your mind, but learn to pay little or no attention to them. They are like trash that floats on the river. You are looking for a strong and sturdy boat. Seek that alone.

Faith is a state of mind that may be induced by self-suggestion. Faith is the antidote for failure. We do not attract what we want but what we are. In order to attract your desire, you must already be in variational alignment with that desire. This is a subtle yet extremely important point. Few understand this important distinction, so few ultimately achieve the wealth and happiness they desire.

> We do not attract what we want
> but what we are.

It's easy to see how *Faith* is the starting point for all accumulation of riches, all success, and all happiness. Given we do not attract what we want but what we are, in order to attract your desire, you must already be in variational alignment with that desire. You must be willing to take a risk and trust in the system. Many people remain too afraid to take the leap of faith required. They fear that it may not work and they will appear foolish.

Have faith that you will achieve your goal, just as you have faith that the sun will rise every morning. This faith need not be spiritual, for the science behind the law of attraction is also highly rational.

Faith will produce a relaxed knowing, a confidence in your future triumph, which all really successful people share. The secret to success lies in not trying too hard. We need to achieve spontaneous performance, and this will only occur when the mind is calm and seems at one with the body.

"*I will believe it when I see it*" is the dictum of the poor masses. The problem, of course, is that doubt or disbelief will start a movement away from you as surely as faith and purpose will start one towards you. Every moment you spend giving heed to your doubts and fears, every moment you spend in worry, every moment in which your soul is possessed by disbelief, sets a current away from you in the whole domain of intelligent substance. The true reality is that: *you will see it when you believe it.*

> The dictum of the poor masses is,
> "I will believe it when I see it."
> Yet the true reality of life is that
> you will see it when you believe it.
> Your ultimate success
> will be determined by
> your willingness to surrender.

In all of this work it is important that you are not distracted. In this regard it is important that you do not pursue other strategies or other concepts in parallel but rather stay focused. If you continually wax and wane from one day to the next, you will create very mixed messages, and the results will be disappointing.

Be crystal clear on what it is you seek. Hold that objective clearly in your mind from one day to the next until it is ultimately achieved. You can then continue the process over and over again by identifying and setting your sights clearly on your next set of objectives.

> In all of this work, it is important
> that you are not distracted
> but stay focused.
> If you continually wax and wane
> from one day to the next,
> you will create
> very mixed messages, and
> the results will be disappointing.
> Be crystal clear
> on what it is you seek.
> Hold that objective clearly in your mind
> from one day to the next
> until it is ultimately achieved.
> You can then continue the process over and over
> again by identifying and setting your sights
> clearly on your next set of objectives.

All thoughts that have been emotionalised (given feeling) and mixed with faith begin immediately to convert themselves into reality. Spend as much of your thinking time as you can in contemplating your picture. The clearer and more definite you make your picture, and the more you dwell upon it, bringing out all its delightful details, the stronger your desire will be. The stronger your desire, the easier it will be to hold your mind fixed upon the picture of what you want.

> *Thoughts that have been emotionalised (given feeling) and mixed with faith begin immediately to convert themselves into reality. Spend as much of your thinking time as you can in contemplating your picture. The more you dwell upon it, bringing out all its delightful details, the quicker the transformation process will be.*

There is a big difference between dreaming about a better life and believing that a better life is already yours, that you are just in the process of receiving it. So do not make the mistake of thinking they are one and the same. They are worlds apart. One entertains and fills in time but delivers no change in your own life. The other turns your dreams into reality.

If in your heart of hearts you still do not truly believe that what you are asking for is realistic or possible, then you are right. You can only receive what you truly believe is your just desert and already on its way to you. Henry Ford, the great industrialist, once said, "If you think you can, you can; if you think you can't, you can't."

If you entertain such doubts, make your request more realistic in your mind. Test the process first on something smaller and more achievable. Slowly build your confidence in the certainty of the process and its ability to work and deliver results. Ask for increasingly more, but never more than you truly believe is possible. Nevertheless, keep in mind that miracles happen every day.

*If, in your heart of hearts,
you do not truly believe that
what you are asking for is realistic or possible,
then you are right.
You can only receive what you truly believe is your
just desert and already on its way to you.
If you think you can, you can;
if you think you can't, you can't.
If this is the case, make your request
more realistic in your mind.
Test the process on something smaller
and more achievable.
Slowly build your confidence
in the certainty of the process
and its ability to work
and deliver you results.
Ask for increasingly more,
but never more than
you truly believe is possible.
Nevertheless, keep in mind that miracles
happen every day.*

If you have not adjusted your life in preparation for what you are about to receive it, is unlikely that it will be delivered. Review once again what it is for which you have asked and ensure that you have taken all the necessary steps to take possession of what you have requested. If not, then act quickly to make the changes necessary to ensure that there are no further barriers between you and your request.

> *If you have not adjusted your life in preparation for what you are about to receive, then you are not in a proper state of readiness to receive what you have requested, and it is unlikely that it will be delivered. Review once again what it is for which you have asked and ensure that you have taken all the necessary steps to take possession of what you have requested. Make the changes necessary to ensure that there are no further barriers between you and your request.*

The problem is that most of us continue to think about what we do not want. Then we wonder why it keeps showing up again and again in our life. Even if we are not intentionally thinking about what is wrong in our life, most of us attract it by default. Our thinking is typically on autopilot, and so everything is typically brought to us by default. So pay more attention to your current thoughts. Change your thinking to focus exclusively on what you want, not on what you currently have.

Thinking about what you do not want will cause it to show up in your life because the Law of Attraction will simply manifest the things about which you are thinking. Life will mirror the dominant thoughts that you think. Where your thinking is on autopilot and in sync with the society or environment in which you currently live, you will simply attract more of the same or more of the bad stuff, as the predominant thought is around what is wrong rather than what is right in the world. Fortunately, there is a time-delay between what you think about and what manifests. That allows you time to reassess your negative thoughts before they become a reality. Change your thinking to focus exclusively on what you want, not what you currently have.

The conscious part of your mind represents only a small part of your mind. The subconscious part of the brain knows how to do a million things perfectly and will do them if you let it.

You must tune in to how you are feeling, as this will give you a good insight to what you are thinking. Pay more attention to your current thoughts.

Finally, a special word on detachment. As difficult as it is to accept, the harder you hang on to something, the less likely you are to keep it. This is another one of the true paradoxes in life, and once again it is rarely understood or followed. Nevertheless, if you want to be successful, you must find the faith and confidence within yourself to trust in the process and detach yourself from the outcome. This doesn't mean that you give up your intention or vision, only your attachment to the result.

> The harder you hang on to something, the less likely you are to keep it. To acquire anything in the physical world, you must first give up your attachment to it. This doesn't mean that you give up your intention or vision, only your attachment to the result.

You will find within yourself two powerful realisations: the power for unlimited potential and the power for unlimited possibility. You are an unlimited spiritual being.

We have a simple formula for success as follows:

BE – DO – HAVE.

Once you define what it is you want to *HAVE*, then you simply need to *BE* a certain type of person and *DO* certain things to achieve those goals.

The story you have just read and its subsequent postscript reveals an important part of the *BE* process in its exploration of **Be**liefs and

Believing. The other key components of **BE**, such as **Be**haviour and **Be**ing, are dealt with in subsequent books in this series.

For now, however, have comfort in the fact that what you have already learned here in these pages has the ability to change your life forever.

THE END

Made in the USA
Monee, IL
25 July 2023